A Day on the Farm

FIRST EDITION
Project Editor Mary Atkinson; **Art Editor** Susan Calver; **Senior Editor** Linda Esposito;
Deputy Managing Art Editor Jane Horne; **US Editor** Regina Kahney; **Production** Kate Oliver;
Picture Researcher Jo Carlill; **Illustrator** Norman Young;
Reading Consultant Linda Gambrell, PhD

THIS EDITION
Editorial Management by Oriel Square
Produced for DK by WonderLab Group LLC
Jennifer Emmett, Erica Green, Kate Hale, *Founders*

Editors Grace Hill Smith, Libby Romero, Michaela Weglinski;
Photography Editors Kelley Miller, Annette Kiesow, Nicole DiMella;
Managing Editor Rachel Houghton; **Designers** Project Design Company;
Researcher Michelle Harris; **Copy Editor** Lori Merritt; **Indexer** Connie Binder;
Proofreader Larry Shea; **Reading Specialist** Dr. Jennifer Albro; **Curriculum Specialist** Elaine Larson

---

Published in the United States by DK Publishing
1745 Broadway, 20th Floor, New York, NY 10019

Copyright © 2023 Dorling Kindersley Limited
DK, a Division of Penguin Random House LLC
23 24 25 26 27 10 9 8 7 6 5 4 3 2 1
001–333434–Apr/2023

All rights reserved.
Without limiting the rights under the copyright reserved
above, no part of this publication may be reproduced, stored
in or introduced into a retrieval system, or transmitted, in any
form, or by any means (electronic, mechanical, photocopying,
recording, or otherwise), without the prior written permission
of the copyright owner.
Published in Great Britain by Dorling Kindersley Limited

A catalog record for this book
is available from the Library of Congress.
HC ISBN: 978-0-7440-6705-7
PB ISBN: 978-0-7440-6706-4

DK books are available at special discounts when purchased
in bulk for sales promotions, premiums, fundraising, or
educational use. For details, contact: DK Publishing Special Markets,
1745 Broadway, 20th Floor, New York, NY 10019
SpecialSales@dk.com

Printed and bound in China

The publisher would like to thank the following for their kind permission to reproduce their images:
a=above; c=center; b=below; l=left; r=right; t=top; b/g=background

Dorling Kindersley: Peter Chadwick / Natural History Museum, London 13cra, 30tl; **Dreamstime.com:** Chanidapha
Charoensuk 26b, Charles Brutlag 15cr, Clara Bastian 16–17, Sue Feldberg 12; **Shutterstock.com:** Danita Delimont 6,
Michael O'Reilly 29, Manasa Qaranivalu 4–5, Kuttelvaserova Stuchelova 15cl

Cover images: *Front:* **Shutterstock.com:** Svitlana Holovei;
Back: **Shutterstock.com:** Ekaterina_Mikhaylova, aliaksei kruhlenia cra

All other images © Dorling Kindersley

For the curious
www.dk.com

A Day on the Farm

Sue Nicholson

Contents

6 Time to Wake Up
16 Time for Lunch
22 Playtime

30 Glossary
31 Index
32 Quiz

Time to Wake Up

It is early in the morning.
The farm is quiet.

Then, the rooster begins to crow.

What a noise!

Cock-a-doodle-doo!

He wakes up all the other farm animals.

In the barn, the mother hen starts to cluck.

One of her eggs is ready to hatch.

Peck, peck, peck!
A tiny chick breaks
through its shell.

shell

More eggs crack open.
Five cheeping chicks
hatch out!

Cheep Cheep
Cheep Cheep

Other farm babies hatch from eggs, too.

The mother duck has six ducklings.

The mother goose has four goslings.

The ducks waddle down to the pond. They take a morning dip.

Their wide, webbed feet push them through the water.

The ducklings have soft, fluffy feathers called "down."

down

Quack

Soon, they will grow long, oily feathers to keep them warm and dry.

Geese like to be near water, too.
The mother goose snaps up grass and weeds in her bright orange bill.

She flaps her wings and honks if anyone comes near her goslings.

Time for Lunch

The cows come to the gate.
It is time for milking!

The farmer milks the cows. The farmer will sell the milk for people to drink.

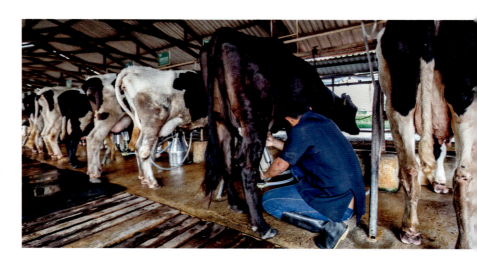

The cows go back to the field to munch grass.

Munch
Munch

17

Other animals are hungry, too.

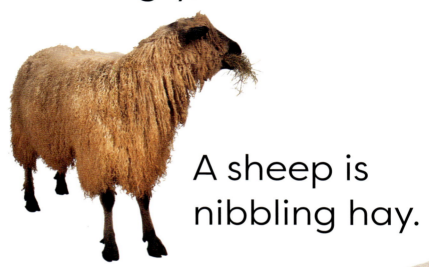

A sheep is nibbling hay.

So is a goat.

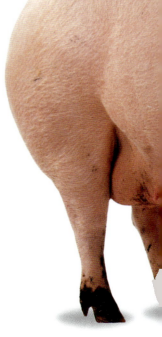

The pigs root around for food in the barn.

One pig has her snout in a bucket of corn!

snout

The farm babies tell their mothers that they are hungry.

"Baa, baa!" cries the lamb to the mother sheep.

"Naa, naa!" cries the kid to the mother goat.

Naa
Naa

The piglets squeal. They drink their mother's milk.

Playtime

Baby animals love to play.
The kids butt each other
with their horns.

horns

The piglets like to roll in the mud.

Out in the fields, the lambs skip and jump. Skip, hop, jump! One tiny hoof follows another.

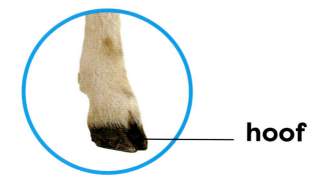

hoof

One calf has lost his mother. "Moo! Moo!" he calls. The mother cow calls back. She is not far away.

Moo Moo

In the afternoon, the sheepdog helps the farmer round up the sheep.

Then, the farmer cuts the wool off the sheep.

The sheep look smaller and cleaner without their wool.

Baa
Baa

wool

Evening comes. It is dark. The farm is quiet.

The chicks, the lambs, and the piglets fall fast asleep.

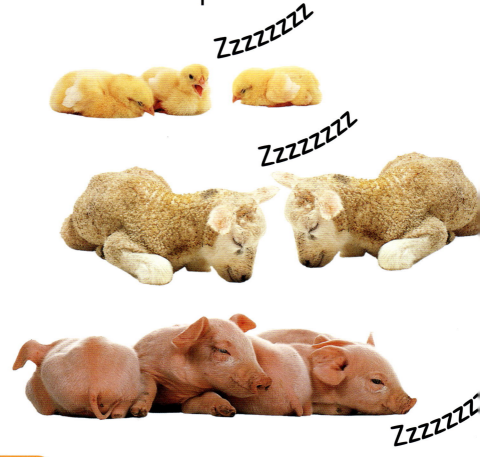

The cat will keep watch until the rooster crows again.

Glossary

down
the small fluffy feathers that keep a bird warm

hoof
the hard part of the foot of some animals

horns
the curved and pointed hard parts on some animals' heads

snout
the long extended nose part of some animals

wool
the thick, soft, curly fur of a sheep or goat

Index

calf 25

cat 29

chicks 9, 28

cows 16, 17, 25

down 13

ducklings 10, 13

ducks 10, 12

eggs 8, 9, 10

farmer 16, 26

goat 18, 21

geese 11, 14

goslings 11, 15

hen 8

kids 21, 22

lambs 20, 24, 28

milk 16, 21

piglets 21, 23, 28

pigs 19

rooster 7, 29

sheep 18, 20, 26, 27

sheepdog 26

wool 26, 27

Quiz

Answer the questions to see what you have learned. Check your answers with an adult.

1. What is a gosling?
2. Why do farmers milk cows?
3. How do piglets like to play?
4. What does the sheepdog do on the farm?
5. Which farm animal is your favorite? What does that animal eat and do at the farm?

1. A baby goose 2. To sell the milk for people to drink
3. They roll in the mud 4. Helps the farmer round up the sheep
5. Answers will vary